STANDING ON THE PROMISES OF GOD

LaTonya R. Forrest

ISBN 978-1-63874-520-4 (paperback)
ISBN 978-1-63874-521-1 (digital)

Christian Faith Publishing
832 Park Avenue
Meadville, PA 16335
www.christianfaithpublishing.com

All scriptures are quoted from the KJV of the Holy Bible.

Printed in the United States of America

To my dad, the late James Edward Forrest, a man of faith who loved God, loved the Word of God, and loved to sing the Word of God. Know that you are greatly missed. But most of all, you are now healed and resting in the arms of Jesus Christ.

CONTENTS

ACKNOWLEDGMENTS

First, I would like to thank God for allowing me the opportunity to share my testimony and minister the Word as an author. All praises, glory, and honor belong to Him. Secondly, I would like to thank my children for their unfailing support. I am who I am because of God and my children.

INTRODUCTION

Oftentimes we spend a lifetime or nearly a lifetime valuing and treasuring people and things, while neglecting ourselves and the gift that lies within us. You go through life assisting others with their goals, dreams, and visions, putting the things that are important to you on the back burner. But what happens when your life begins to shift and your tests and trials begin to push you into your God-ordained purpose? What happens when that thing that God has placed inside you begins to nag at you, pull on you, and overtake your thoughts? What happens when you are no longer needed and friends and family begin to turn their backs on you? You face rejection, fear, and disappointment. What happens when you find yourself on your face, lying prostrate before the Lord, and He shows you who you are in Him? What happens when the Lord tells you He is sending you to a rebellious people, a people who will not hear (listen)? "Thou dwellest in the midst of a rebellious house which have eyes to see, and see not; they have ears but hear not: for they are a rebellious house" (Ezekiel 12:2).

Yet the Lord promises to heal, restore, and bless you, your children, and your children's children if you would seek the face of God, turn from sin, accept Jesus as your Lord and personal Savior, worship Him in spirit and in truth, and stop worshipping idols (people and stuff). I trust God. I believe God. I trust His plan. I stand on the promises of God.

CHAPTER 1

My Childhood

I grew up in the projects on the west side of Chicago. I lived there for fourteen years. I was four years old when my family moved there, and I left after I turned eighteen years of age and had graduated from high school. My mother and father did not have much. But we had each other, and we had the Lord. My mother was a God-fearing woman. And she surely instilled the fear of the Lord in us. There were several things my mother would teach us throughout life that have always stuck with me. One of them is this: just because you lived in the projects does not mean you have to act like the projects. My mother expected us to carry ourselves with a certain level of decency and dignity. She did not expect us to act like the environment in which we were being raised. She wanted her children to excel despite of and beyond their environment. I definitely understood her perspective. People who grew up in or lived in the projects were considered poor, some criminals, and were not expected to go far in life or even live a long life, for that matter. While this may be true to some degree, it is not absolute. I do know a lot of successful people who came from the projects and didn't become a product of their environment. Another saying my mother continuously preached was if we messed up and got pregnant out of wedlock, we better not get rid of the baby. She often would reflect on the story of a woman who had so many abortions that she had begun to hear the cry of those babies. Another lesson she repeatedly spoke on was to be careful with who you have children with. She often reflected on the blood type of both parents. She would always tell the story of how back in her day, if a man and woman's blood types did not go together or weren't compatible, then they weren't allowed to get married. She would say that if the blood type did not go together, then something would be wrong with the baby. Ironically, I actually ended up going through this. My last two children were ABO incompatible, meaning I had children by someone whose blood type was not compatible with mine, and my children ended up needing blood transfusions. Because of my mother's teachings, I was familiar with what was happening with my children. Because my mother instilled the fear of the Lord in me, I knew it was better to keep my children despite having them out of wedlock. As a young girl, I listened and heard the sayings of my mother. I took her teachings to heart. I wanted to do all I could to please my parents. I wanted to make my parents proud. Pleasing my parents was the goal. And I lived most of my life trying to do just that. This may sound nice, but it had both positive and negative effects.

Though I wanted to please my parents, I ultimately did not live to please myself, which had an effect on my emotions later in life. We will talk about that later in this book. I was the fifth child, middle child, and first girl but often felt like I was the oldest child. I had nine other siblings, five brothers and four sisters.

I closely watched my mother take care of business. She also taught me how to take care of business. I often felt like it was my responsibility to make sure everything was all right. I was my mom's right-hand person. I was fine with that because I loved my parents and wanted to make sure everyone and everything was all right, even if it meant me sacrificing my own happiness.

CHAPTER 2

Separation

In December 2012, my father passed away. Oh, how I miss him. After the passing of my father, I went through a period of separation from my mother. I had become used to being there for pretty much everything she needed. When she called, I was there. A lot of times I would volunteer my time because I just wanted to be there for her and my father. But since my father had passed, things had begun to change. I was no longer needed. This was very difficult for me to accept because I had become accustomed to being there. So I began to try to force the relationship. In forcing the relationship, I began to face rejection. Yes, from my mother. I do not believe that she did this intentionally. Neither am I writing this to bring any type of condemnation or shame to my mother. I have a great mother, and she raised me well.

However, in this season of separation, I believe the Lord allowed her to reject me from coming around and doing things for her. My mother was widowed and maybe somehow felt free, and now she wanted to do things on her own and with other people. This somehow made me feel used, believe it or not. But I had to accept the change regardless of how I felt about it.

I now had to figure out how to live my life without my father and with my mother's newfound freedom, pretty much without her. It was painful. At the same time, I had to realize the purpose of the separation. When God is bringing you into the place that He would have for you to be in, it requires separation. Everyone cannot go with you.

It was really hard to accept the fact that I was being separated physically and emotionally from my mother. But deep down inside, I knew it was God's will and that I had to accept what was happening in my life. After all, it was not in my control anyway. I could not change the feelings of my mother at that time, and it was causing friction in our relationship. Though separation may bring about negative emotions, separation is not always negative. In fact, separation is necessary. Despite the reason for separation in any relationship, know that it is happening for a reason and ultimately will put you in alignment with the people you are meant to be around in that season. Even if that season requires no one but you and God. Though I wanted to be there for my mother, she no longer desired my presence. I picked up and moved to the suburbs. I had moved closer to my mom for several reasons: to be there for her and to look after her. She was also my childcare provider, and my dad provided the transportation. Since the passing of my father, this had come to an end, and it was simply time to move on. On top of that, I had other issues that played into the move. Such as having boys and being concerned for their safety and survival in the city of Chicago, my call to ministry, and simply wanting better for my family and myself. I now had an opportunity to make a move that was most beneficial to the health of my family. I pretty much knew what suburb I wanted to live in. So I began my search for a home to rent. While I was searching, I ran into this home that popped up on a realty website and inquired within minutes of the posting. I reached out to the property management and was literally the first applicant. I prayed about it, and the Holy Spirit told me it was mine. My family and I went to view the property, and we got it.

God kept His promise. There has never been a time that God had made me a promise He did not keep. He is a promise keeper. He may not have given me everything that I asked for, but He has been a provider for my children and me. He has been a waymaker and continues to make a way even when there seems to be no way. That is why you don't have to fret over who left you, disappointed you, or who turned their back on you. Jesus made me a promise. He promised me that He will never leave me or forsake me. I stand on that. Life may have not been easy, but Jesus has never left me. Times may have been rough, and my family and I have been through some unfavorable situations. But we made it because of Jesus. Jesus kept His word. He has never left me. Sometimes we mistake our storms for abandonment. Jesus will not leave you in your storm. He is right there. Because of our human nature, we sometimes have a problem of accepting what God allows, and sometimes what God allows does not feel good in the flesh or in the natural. But know that your storm or circumstance did not catch God by surprise. He knew what was going to happen before it happened, and He knows what the outcome is going to be. Our job is to go through and trust that He is there, steering the boat, preserving and keeping you, strengthening you, growing you, maturing you, making you better for His glory.

I am reminded of the story of Job where the sons of God were meeting with the Lord and Satan was present. When I read this, to my own surprise, I laughed a little. I asked myself, "Why did you laugh at this?" But I know why I laughed. I laughed because the devil had the nerve to show up among the righteous. Yes, Satan was right there among the righteous. "And the Lord said unto Satan, Whence comest thou? Then Satan answered the Lord, and said, From going to and fro in the earth, and from walking up and down in it. And the Lord said unto Satan, Hast thou considered my servant Job" (Job1:7–8). Notice how God described Job. Job was a servant. Job was an upright man who feared God and hated evil. God gave the devil permission to strike all of Job's possessions but to spare his life. "Satan questioned the Lord, Hast not thou made an hedge about him, and about his house and about all that he hath on every side?" (Job 1:10). You see, the devil could not touch Job because the Lord had a hedge of protection around Job. So the Lord removed the hedge of protection from around Job to allow the attack of the enemy. The devil was allowed to attack all that Job had. But the devil did not have permission to take Job's life. The devil just knew that if he took everything Job had that Job would curse God. But Job was an upright, wealthy man who had favor with the Lord. Despite Job losing everything, He did not curse God. Instead, in Job 1:21, Job said, "Naked came I out of my mother's womb, and naked shall I return thither: the Lord gave, and the Lord hath taken away; blessed be the name of the Lord." After the devil saw that Job did not curse God, Satan presented himself again among the righteous. The Lord said unto Satan, "From whence comest thou?" And Satan answered the Lord, saying, "From going to and fro in the earth, and from walking up and down it." And the Lord asked Satan, "Have you considered my servant,

Job, who fears God, hates evil, and walks in integrity even though you have moved me against him, to destroy him without cause?" Satan then challenged God and said, "But put forth thine hand now, and touch his bone and his flesh, and he will curse thee to thy face." The Lord said to Satan, "He is in thine hand; but save his life" (Job 2:2–6). Satan smote Job with sore boils from the crown of his head to the sole of his feet. Yet Job maintained his integrity and did not sin with his lips. He did not curse God. Because of Job's faithfulness, the Lord blessed Job with double of what he had lost. How many of us can say that if we were tried like Job, if you lost everything in one day, including your wife/husband, children, your wealth, and your health, that you would not curse God? I have to be honest. I myself have not always had the mindset to just trust God. That came after a period of trials and submission to the will of God. Every attack is not a consequence of disobedience. Some things God allows to happen in your life because He knows that He can trust you. He can trust you to remain faithful. God will allow some things to happen to you because He knows that you can handle it. He wants to use your testimony for His glory. He wants to use you to encourage someone else and let others know that if God did it for you, then He can do it for them. If God has blessed you, He is able to bless the next person. If God has healed you, He can heal the next person. If God has kept you, He can keep the next person. He will keep your children. He will keep your mind. He can change your heart. He can heal your body. He is a mind regulator. He is a provider. He is a waymaker. He is a restorer. God can restore back to you everything you have lost, only better. God will never put more on you than you can bear. And just in case you get angry and slip, that's where God's grace and mercy kicks in. All you have to do is repent (sincerely). God is faithful and just to forgive.

Sometimes I often feel like Job. Job suffered much. Not because he had sinned but because he was faithful. Every suffering is not a result of sin but a battle of good vs. evil. The Lord knew he could trust Job. That is why he gave the devil permission to test him. The Lord will never put more on you than you can bear. Neither will he allow you to go through any situation that you cannot handle. But He has to try you and see if He can trust you. Can God trust you with double? Or will we turn our backs on God as soon as we do not get what we want? Job was a wealthy man and in one day lost everything he had. But he trusted God. I do not know about you, but I believe God. If God said He would give me double for my trouble, then I believe God. God is looking for faithful servants who will trust Him. Not just for what He promised that you can have. But because He's God and my Father owns the cattle on a thousand hills.

The devil, on the other hand, just wants the opportunity to embarrass and mock the life of a Christian and keep people from believing that God is who He says He is. And that is everything. God is everything you need. God can do anything. The devil wants you to believe that it does not pay to serve Jesus. He wants the opportunity to go back to the Lord and laugh and brag and tell God, "I told you he/she was not faithful." Our job in our Christian walk is to remain faithful so someone else might believe that God is a rewarder of those who diligently seek Him. Give the devil a black eye and keep trusting God.

How many times has God spoken a promise to you or given you a peace that everything was going to be all right but you became impatient and frustrated right before God brought the promise to pass? That has happened to me quite a bit in life. However, I learned from it. First, I would feel guilty immediately because I knew God had made me a promise. Why did I not fully trust Him? How could I give up on God? All I had to do was wait a little longer; God already had it covered. Oftentimes we get frustrated because it seems like God is taking too long to bring His promise to pass. Just as soon as I become upset, God comes through for me. Another emotion I felt was shame. I would get frustrated, then God would immediately prove Himself to me. Each incident taught me to trust God more and more and to take His word for it. Allow God to prove Himself to you. If God made you a promise, He will bring it to pass.

CHAPTER 3

Waiting on God

"But they that wait upon the Lord shall renew their strength; they shall mount up with wings as eagles; they shall run, and not be weary; and they shall walk, and not faint" (Isaiah 40:31).

"Wait, I say, on the Lord"(Psalm 27:14).

Waiting can be the most difficult thing to do. Oftentimes we want a yes. Sometimes the answer is no. But what do you do when the Lord says to wait? Waiting on the Lord is not the same as a no. It is natural or human nature to mistake wait for a no.

Oftentimes our actions can be driven by anxiety or fear of the unknown. Sometimes our circumstances can force us into positions where we feel like we have to make sudden moves to make things happen. Timing is everything. But it is important that our actions are not driven by fear or anxiety but by the word of God and the unction of the Holy Spirit. What I mean by that is that my emotions may tell me to decide right away, but deep down inside I feel the Holy Spirit quietly saying, "Wait on me." It is okay to do all you can. But as the song by Donnie McClurkin states, "After you have done all you can, you just stand." Stand still and see the salvation of the Lord. Often we like to take matters into our own hands when the Lord is clearly saying, "Trust me, son. Trust me, daughter. I got you." To trust God, you have to have the faith to believe that God will do just what He said he will do. He may not come when you want Him to, but one thing is for sure: God is always on time. His Word says, "I have never seen the righteous forsaken nor his seed begging for bread." God will never leave you nor forsake you. Sometimes the wait feels just like that. That God has forgotten you. But His word tells me that he will be with me always, even until the end of the world. So when God tells us to wait, we have to trust that He, the Most High, has our best interest in mind. There are several reasons why the Lord may tell you to wait.

Protection. "For I know the thoughts that I think toward you, saith the Lord, thoughts of peace, and not of evil, to give you an expected end" (Jeremiah 29:11). God has a plan for each and every one of our lives. But when we refuse to listen to God and go before God, we disrupt his plan. Sometimes God requires us to wait because he is protecting us. God knows what lies ahead of us and there are just some things that he does not want his children to endure. This is called divine protection. God is always protecting his children from dangers seen and unseen. God knows about the traps and difficulties that lies ahead that could hinder or possibly cause you to miss your purpose and His promise. God tells us to wait to protect us. He loves his children.

Preparation. There were times when I was anxious about going into ministry. Then there were times when I felt like I myself was not ready. Though I at times have felt like I was not good enough, God would test and show me and use people and circumstances to assure me that yes, I was good enough. However, there was a preparation period. Though I knew I was called, I faced a lot of adversity.

I faced adversity within my family and at work. Honestly, I faced adversity in every area of life. I knew the hand of the Lord was on my life and through adversity I was being tried and tested. The Lord was teaching me, training me, growing me, and stretching me. One thing about it is if you are going to do this thing called ministry, you have to develop tough skin. The Lord was teaching me through opposition how to stand and endure.

Out of season. There is an appointed time for God to bring you into the things He has for you. God's timing is perfect. When you wait on your season, whatever God has called you to, He has also prepared you to do it. And it shall be fruitful. It shall be profitable. It will work. Going out of season puts you in the wrong place at the wrong time. Moving out of season can cause you to miss out on what God really has for you. I do not know about you, but I need everything God has for me.

I am a single mother: I actually tried to use this as an excuse to escape my call to ministry. But, of course, it did not work. The Lord allowed me to minister in front of my kids and with my kids. As a matter of fact, I somehow ended up teaching in children's church. Being a single parent does not excuse the call that God has on your life. Whatever it is that God has created you to do, He will make a way or provision for you to accomplish what He gave you to do despite your situation, despite your circumstances, and despite your mistakes. As long as you have repented and have chosen to walk in obedience, you will obtain the favor of God. We serve a God who is great and mighty, who does all things well. He will perfect that which is concerning you. He will make the crooked places straight.

Wisdom/revelation. I did not always understand the wait. Why did I have to wait? God had shown me a piece of the vision, and I was excited and ready to go. The problem wasn't that I wasn't ready but that the door was not always open. I was not always received or accepted. Therefore, I had to wait. As I looked to my left and my right, it appeared as if everyone was moving toward their destiny. People were being promoted, blessed, ordained, married, etc. But I had to wait. And that is okay because when your door does open, no man can shut it. No man will be able to stop what God is doing in your life.

When you wait on your season, God can clearly reveal to you what it is that He is requiring of you or wants you to do. Revelation will put you directly in alignment with the will that God has for your life. Not my will but thy will be done.

CHAPTER 4

Rejection

I have dealt with rejection on so many levels. Growing up I never felt like I belonged. I never felt like I was a part of the in crowd. As a matter of fact, I knew I was not a part of the in crowd. Some people made it known. Some did not. But I knew I was not popular. Maybe known a little bit, but not popular. Honestly, I was okay with that. By nature I was a loner. I did not care much for unnecessary relationships. Neither did I like phony people. The crowd does not excite me. So some levels of rejection did not bother me. On the other hand, other levels did.

Rejection from family can be very painful. Even growing up I knew I was different from my siblings. My sisters use to ridicule me and say that I was so serious. They would laugh and giggle all the time. And me, I could never figure out what was so funny. They just giggled a lot. That was irritating to me. Even as adults, they still make jokes at the family gatherings and would make comments such as, "Tonya has always been so serious," and would keep right on laughing. Sometimes my feelings would be just a little bit hurt because they were right. I have always been too serious to laugh. Throughout the years, I have gotten better, and I am learning to laugh again.

On a deeper level, I experience rejection from my mom. As I stated in the beginning of the book, I've lived a life trying to please my parents. Therefore, I gave a lot of myself and neglected my own desires or put my plans on the back burner to ensure that my parents were taken care of, all to eventually be rejected by my mother. I do not tell this story to bring any shame or humiliation to my parents nor my family. I have an awesome, virtuous mother who did all she could to raise us right. She did a phenomenal job. However, I am sharing this because it is a part of my story, and I am sure someone else may have experienced this type of rejection. Even from family. You are not alone. As a matter of fact, I believe this is just the way the Lord had my mother fixed concerning me for a season. Nothing happens by happenstance. Everything happens for a reason. In my situation, I believe it was because God was bringing me into a period of isolation. I was being prepared for ministry. No matter how much you love your family, be it mother, father, sister, or brother, when God calls you, He is calling you. Everyone cannot go with you. Everyone will not be assigned to help you. Everyone will not be happy for you. Neither will everyone be in your corner. But one thing you can be sure of is God is with you.

Rejection in Intimate Relationships

I have experienced rejection a few times in my life. It mainly happened due to my disobedience. It is very important to have discernment in any relationship. It is also very important to identify the type of relationship and level of the relationship. Any relationship without identity is simply a waste of time. I have spent time on people who have literally drained me mentally, physically, and spiritually. It turned out to be a waste of time. Honestly, people are not always necessarily attracted to you but to the idea of you. Maybe not even the idea of you but the oil on you. I was once talking to someone who said I was anointed for them. That may have been true. But I was not anointed to be with the person. I was mainly anointed to help that person through a particular situation. God did give me the discernment to walk away. But because I had not been in an actual relationship in a long time, I disobeyed God.

In disobeying God, I ended up rejected and on the altar. Obedience is definitely better than sacrifice. It is important to be able to identify the relationship, and when God says the season is up, walk away.

In my disobedience, I found myself being more and more physically and spiritually drained. Being a person who is sensitive to the spirits of others, I can sense when things were not so right, or when I would pick up some things in the spirit, I would call this individual. Well, needless to say, eventually this person began to reject me. Once I prayed and coached him back onto his feet, he no longer had a need for me. Because I did not remove myself from the relationship when God told me to, I ended up broken. I, however, thank God because through prayer and lessons from past experiences, this opened my eyes even more to the importance of obedience. Had I just obeyed the voice of the Lord, I would not have gone through that pain. Despite the pain, I learned to trust the voice of the Lord even more. If God is telling you to walk away from a relationship, situation, a person, place, or thing, know that He has your best interest in mind. He knows what lies ahead. God knows what is best for you. His plan is not to harm or hurt you but to give you hope and a future, to bring you to an expected end (Jeremiah 29:11). This simply means God has a plan for your life, and His plan is perfect. His plan is to bless you, not to harm you. Sometimes we are so busy trying to hold on to that toxic or unhealthy relationship that God told you to walk away from weeks, months, or years ago that you miss out on the relationship (that husband, that wife, that friendship, that business partner, or that divine connection) God really has for you.

CHAPTER 5

Isolation

Being rejected often pushed me into isolation. I have had quite a few seasons of isolation. In a sense, having to stay inside due to the COVID-19 pandemic was not completely horrible for me. Due to my seasons of isolation, being out of the church for a time and in the presence of the Lord was not totally new to me. It is during isolation that I truly improve my relationship with the Lord. Oftentimes we look at our circumstances, situations, and disappointments as horrible events in our lives when actually, God allows certain things to happen to us to draw us back to Him or to draw us closer to Him. If we can all be honest, we do not run to God as much when things are going well in our lives. But we tend to cry out to God when our lives are under distress. God is not looking for a part-time lover. He is looking for those who will worship Him in season and out of season, when times are good and when times are bad, in spirit and in truth. God wants to have a relationship with you that is genuine, not convenient.

Each season of isolation has taught me different things. Though the situations were different, they all sent me back to the same God. The God of all. The God of love. The God that delivers. The God that heals. The God that sets free. And the God that fights for us.

One situation that led me into isolation was fighting to maintain custody of my children. Back in 2010, I left a both verbally and physically abusive relationship for good. After putting this man out of my house for good, he filed for custody of the children. Not visitation custody. I have been in and out of court for nearly ten years fighting to maintain custody of my children. Because I no longer accepted the abuse, the devil was coming for my family. But through my processes, the Lord promised me that He would never leave me nor forsake me. He promised me that He would cover and protect my children. Despite the promise, no matter how hard I fought in court and out of court for my children, it always appeared that I was on the losing end. The court was not concerned about the abuse that I had endured in the past. They were concerned about the present. Despite my attempts to prove that the father had not changed, the court did not care. All they appeared to care about was the children seeing their father. Not child support, not the safety of the children, nor the father's ability to provide for his children. No matter how I have prayed, this situation has not gone anywhere.

I've questioned God, "How long should the wicked prevail? Lord, when are you going to deliver me out of this situation?" God's response was, "Wait for it." God will punish the wicked in His own timing.

Someone once told me that my job or assignment was to draw this person to Christ by exemplifying love. Though I know that it is not God's will that anyone should perish. This person appears to be the devil's advocate. Personally, I see this person as a thorn in my flesh. We all have a thorn. We all have something that we have prayed for the Lord to remove from our lives. But if you and I were honest, it is the thorn that gives you the push, the reason, the motivation to walk in your purpose. Yes, even that problem that just will not go away has a purpose in your life. The Lord would give me the scripture Psalm 37:1–2: "Fret not thyself because of evildoers neither be thou envious against the workers of iniquity. For they shall soon be cut down like the grass, and wither as the green herb." In these scriptures, God is telling us to not worry about those who do evil against us. Do not be jealous because their evil ways appear to prosper. The promise is that they will soon be cut down and will exist no more and will not be remembered. The instruction and promise are also in the third and fourth verse of Psalm 37: "Trust in the Lord, and do good, so shalt thou dwell in the land, and verily thou shalt be fed. Delight thyself also in the Lord, and he shall give thee the desires of thine heart." Here David (the author of the book of Psalm) is saying, "Take your focus off of the evildoer and focus on what God wants you to do. If we focus on God and what He wants us to do, then God will give us the desires of our heart."

Despite what I was going through, God did not want me to focus on the battle. He wanted me to focus on Him. God had another plan in mind. There were times when I wanted to fight, but that was not God's will. Instead of fighting with the system, the Lord wanted me to fight with prayer. In the midst of prayer, the Lord was teaching me to endure. I would constantly hear the Lord telling me,

"I'm teaching you something." God was and still is teaching me to surrender. Surrendering lets God know that we trust Him to handle the situation. Surrendering removes my hand from the situation so that I can allow God to fix the problem His way and in His timing. My job is to obey and trust Him.

CHAPTER 6

My Calling

The Lord called me to ministry at the age of thirty. During this time, I was not living a saved life. Though I was raised in church and loved God, I was still living in sin. There were some areas I had improved on, but God was definitely dealing with me concerning my sin. I was a fornicator. And while one sin is no bigger than another, sin is sin, and God was not pleased. Every time I opened my Bible, God was speaking to me telling me not to fornicate. It was as if the Bible had come to life and God was speaking directly to me. And you know what? He was. Every time I went to fornicate, God would speak to me about this particular man

I was seeing and told me, "Do not fornicate." I could hear the voice of the Lord right before committing the sin, telling me not to fornicate. Then the voice would speak, "So you are going to do it anyway?"

I clearly knew that God was telling me not to commit this sin. Even though I did it, God would still deal with me and have me on my face. Telling me that I was like the children of Israel, warning me not to do as my fathers have done.

While God was convicting me of my sins, He was reminding me of His promises. Just as sin came with a price, so does obedience. God would constantly remind me of the blessings of obedience and the curses of disobedience. The entire chapter 11 of Deuteronomy speaks about the blessings of obedience, curses of disobedience, and the promises of God for your obedience. But I will just elaborate a little on what stood out for me: Deuteronomy 11:8–9, which quotes, "Therefore shall ye keep all the commandments which I command you this day, that ye may be strong, and go in and possess the land, whither ye go to possess it; And that ye may prolong your days in the land, which the Lord sware unto your fathers to give unto them and to their seed, a land that floweth with milk and honey." Here in these two verses, God is telling us that if we keep His commandments (obedience), He would provide us with the strength to possess the land (the promise). Not only that, but God promises long life in the land and land that flows with milk and honey (blessings of abundance, plenty, more than enough).

Not only does God promise to bless you and me, later in Deuteronomy 11:19–21, He promises to bless our children. I don't know about you, but I want to receive the promise. I want the blessing. I want my seed (children) to be blessed.

Not only was God calling me out from a life of sin, but He was also calling me into a life of ministry. When I first heard the call to ministry or had my encounter, the Lord told me to preach, teach, and teach my children. I looked over my shoulder. Of course, no one was there but me. I questioned God. "Me?" The Lord told me to preach, teach, and teach my children. I have always taught my children. Just as my mom had always taught us. I believe in raising children in the fear of the Lord and teaching them right from wrong.

I believe in teaching my children to work hard for whatever they want, especially my boys. No one owes you anything. I teach my children to put their best foot forward every time. I encourage my children to walk in the area of gifting and calling that God has placed on their lives. I also push my children to go further than me in life. To be better than me. Every parent should want to see their seed exceed them. Each generation should become better than the last. I also teach my children to live morally correct lives. To do what's right even when no one is looking. It does not matter what you do when I am looking. Your true character is in what you do when I am not looking. I teach my children to honor and revere God and to put God first in everything they do.

Most of all, I do my best to live it before them. I do my best to live the life that I sing and pray about. The best thing you can do for your children is be an example for them.

Now, back to my call to ministry. I kept having these encounters, and the Lord would have me lie prostrate on my face and showed me visions. For a few years, I had a hard time accepting what I had heard the Lord speak to me. I knew I was different. I knew I could not do what everybody else did. I knew I could not do wrong and get away with it. I knew I hated to see people get bullied or mistreated. But I can honestly say that I did not know I was called to preach until the age of thirty. Unfortunately, I do not have the testimony of knowing I was called from a young child or a teenager. Sometimes I wonder if I was just naive and was not paying attention to what God was doing in my life. I do know I used to have a lot of dreams and déjà vus. As a child, I remember saying often, "I've seen this before."

At first, I was not okay with this. I was not okay with being called to preach, and at the age of thirty years old too. Most people have the testimony of being called at a young age. I was thirty years old. I had different emotions. I felt fearful. I felt unworthy. After all, I had had four children out of wedlock. Who was I going to preach to? I did not have much. Why didn't I know before now? But the Lord would not leave me alone. He kept showing up and telling me I was called to preach. Then He would begin to convict me and tell me I had not done what He told me to do. Honestly, this put even more of a fear in me for the Lord. Despite how I felt about being called to ministry, God was calling me. And I needed to at least attempt to answer the call. Despite the fear I had of ministry, of speaking to people, even strangers, God was speaking through me to people. It is as if He was sitting on my shoulders, whispering in my ear, telling me exactly what to say to the people. If I obeyed, it was well. If I disobeyed, it would weigh on me as if I had disappointed God. After I repented, God would usually send the same test again to give me an opportunity to do what He told me to do. If I can be honest, it was easier to do what God told me to do vs. bearing the guilt of not doing what He told me to do. I would know when the voice I was hearing was God because whoever He sent me to minister to would receive the word. Even if they didn't want to initially, they had to yield to the power of the Holy Ghost.

The more I obeyed, the easier it became to obey (not in all cases). I hated the feeling of guilt or conviction when disobeying God. I felt as if I had let Him down. Furthermore, I hated the thought that someone's life could be predicated on my willingness to obey God. Your obedience can be the difference between someone living or dying both physically and spiritually. God would remind me through scripture of the importance of obedience and the consequences of disobedience.

When I say unto the wicked, Thou shalt surely die; and thou givest him not warning, nor speakest to warn the wicked from his wicked way, to save his life; the same wicked man shall die in his iniquity; but his blood will I require at thine hand. Yet if thou warn the wicked, and he turn not from his wickedness, nor from his wicked way, he shall die in his iniquity; but thou hast delivered thy soul. Again, When a righteous *man* doth turn from his righteousness, and commit iniquity, and I lay a stumbling block before him, he shall die: because thou hast not given him warning, he shall die in his sin, and his righteousness which he hath done shall not be remembered; but his blood will I require at thine hand. Nevertheless if thou warn the righteous *man*, that the righteous sin not, and he doth not sin, he shall surely live, because he is warned; also, thou hast delivered thy soul. (Ezekiel 3:18–21)

If I were to break these scriptures down into simplicity, what the scripture is saying in Ezekiel 3:18–21 is this: if God has told you to speak to someone who is not saved and give them warning so that their soul may be saved and you do not do it, and that person dies in their sin, then their blood is on your hands.

However, if you do warn a sinner and he/she does not turn from their wicked ways and he/she dies in their iniquity, God will not hold you responsible for that person's death because you have done what God has told you to do. The twentieth verse speaks about the righteous. When a righteous man turns away from a lifestyle of righteous into sin and you did not correct him and that righteous man dies, his righteousness is forgotten. And his soul is lost because you did not warn or correct him. That blood is on your hands.

However, if you warn or correct the righteous man and he does not sin, he will live (verse 21). I believe this is pertaining to a death both physically and spiritually.

I know these scriptures may sound scary, harsh, and may almost feel like damnation. Like I am destined to die for disobedience. Listen, when I first read those scriptures, I was afraid. The last thing I wanted was anybody's blood on my hands. Why had God chosen me for such a difficult task? Know that when God calls you to anything, He already knows your fears and the level of your fears. But your fear is not going to stop Him from calling you. However, your fear can prevent you from answering the call. Saying yes does not remove the fear. However, saying yes to whatever calling God has for your life shows your love, your reverence, your honor, your respect, and your submission to the will of God for your life. When you say yes to the call, you are telling God, "Despite of the fear I have, despite of the way I feel, I trust you. I trust you, Lord, to make provision for the vision. I trust you to cover me in all my ways. I trust you, Lord, for the process. I trust you, Lord, for the promise. And most of all, I trust you, Lord, with my life." God is not going to punish you because you are afraid to do what He told you to do. Moving from fear and walking in God's will is a process, and God knows where you are in the process and will continue to develop you in your process. The key is to obey despite your fear. When we submit to God's will, we are giving our life back to Him, for our life is not our own. It belongs to God. When we give our life back to God, He can get the glory out of our life. We in return reap the benefits of belonging to Him, honoring Him, serving Him, and worshiping Him.

Know that whatever calling God has placed on your life is there for a purpose. Your calling is designed to fulfill a need in the earthly realm. Know that whatever God has called you to do is needed. Someone is waiting on what you have inside you to push them to their next level, to warn them, to encourage them, to motivate them, to lead them to salvation, to keep them saved, to educate them, or even to save someone's life. Whatever call or assignment God has given you, it is necessary.

God will not send you to a place without equipping you to fulfill the assignment. Your trials, your tests, your mistakes, your experiences all equip you for the assignment.

Overcoming People

Overcoming people has got to be one of the hardest things that I have ever had to do. I'm not going to elaborate on this topic much because it's such a process. But if you are looking for validation from people, stop it. You are looking in the wrong place. Overcoming people is critical to walking in your purpose. People will talk about you, chastise you, and criticize you. It really doesn't matter what you do when it comes down to what people think of you. You can never please everyone, and someone will always have something negative to say. If you allow the thoughts of people to resonate in your spirit, you will never fully become who

God created you to be and you will never obtain the promise. You will never reach your goal. People are always going to have something to say. But who do you believe? I choose to believe God and stand on the promises of God. Even in writing this book, I often hesitated because at times I worried about what people would think of me as they read it. But again, the Lord had to deal with me concerning obedience. As I get older and mature from different trials and tests, I learned obedience is so much better than sacrifice. Many times I fell into depression (not clinically diagnosed), but if I would be honest with myself, I fell into depression. Feeling too sorry for myself to get up and take a shower, lying in my bed worrying about rejection, fear, and what people would think about me. Who am I to minister to anyone? Who am I that I can tell anyone how they should live? Writing this book is one of the calls God has placed in my life. I choose to obey. Doing what God has called you to do will not always be the glamorous thing to do. It will not always be comfortable. It may not be the popular thing to do. It may cause you to lose some friends and maybe even some family relationships. But the most important thing is that you obeyed God.

CHAPTER 8

Obedience

Once you overcome people, you are free to walk in obedience. Obedience gets God's attention. God responds to your obedience. Deutoromony 6:1-4 quotes:

> Now these are the commandments, the statutes, and the judgments, which the Lord your God commanded to teach you, that ye might do them in the land whither ye go to possess it: That thou mightest fear the Lord thy God, to keep all his statutes and his commandments,

which I command thee, thou, and thy son, and thy son's son, all the days of thy life; and that thy days may be prolonged. Hear therefore, O Israel, and observe to do it; that it may be well with thee, and that ye may increase mightily, as the Lord God of thy fathers hath promised thee, in the land that floweth with milk and honey.

When you, me, or we obey the will of God, He has to respond. He has to keep His promise. The promises of God are "Yea" and "Amen." But the condition to obtaining the promise is obedience.

Will you answer the call? When I ask this, I am referring to whatever call God has placed in your life. I do not know what God has placed in your heart to do, but whatever it is, do it. Ministry is not just preaching. Ministry is not confined to the walls of the church. Ministry is everywhere. Ministry is in your home. Ministry is in your job. Ministry is the way we conduct ourselves in stressful situations. Ministry is in how we treat one another. Ministry is being kind. Ministry is showing love. Do you know that love covers a multitude of sin? If we would learn to show love, imagine how many people we could bring to Christ. Love covers a multitude of sin. Ministry is in what we say and how we say it. Ministry is in what we do.

CHAPTER 9

Fear

> For God has not given us the spirit of fear but
>
> of power, and of love, and of a sound mind.
>
> —2 Timothy 1:7

Fear will arise when you are walking or attempting to walk in obedience. But you have to be careful not to let fear cripple you and cause you to become stagnant. Fear will cause you to miss out on obtaining your promise. Fear will magnify negative thoughts and cause you to believe that the promise is not obtainable. Don't allow fear to prevent you from stepping out on faith and accomplishing the things that God has for you to do.

Sometimes we experience failure after failure because we are trying to do things that do not line up with God's will for our lives. Do not allow disobedience to hinder your blessings. I don't want to die with my purpose in me.

Do not let your obstacles prevent you from obtaining the blessings that God has for you. We all have trials and tests. But know that if God brought you to it, He will surely bring you through it. He has given you the power and authority to possess the land.

Familiarity is not going to get it! Step outside the boat. Obtaining the promise would require you to step outside of your comfort zone, to step out on faith and do something that you have never done before. The scriptures tell us, "Now, Faith is the substance of things hope for and the evidence of things not seen" (Hebrew 1:1). For Abraham to receive the promise, he had to leave his place of familiarity. He had to leave the place he'd known and sojourn to a place he had not seen. That required him to first believe the promise that God made him. God told Abraham that he was going to possess the land, be the father of many nations, that his seed could not be numbered, and that his seed is blessed (Genesis 12:1). For Peter to walk on water like Jesus, he had to get out of the boat. He had to leave a place that he presumed was safe to get to Jesus. And you know what? Peter did do the impossible; he walked on water. It wasn't until Peter feared the wind and began to doubt that he began to sink. Then Jesus reached out and saved him. Know that you have the ability to do what seems impossible, but it requires faith. Faith would require you to move even when you don't know the outcome. Without faith, it is impossible to please the Lord. Without faith, it is impossible to stand on His word. Without faith, it is impossible to stand on the promises of God.

CHAPTER 10

Discouragement/Closed Doors

I have had so many situations or incidents that discouraged me from walking in my calling. When I professed to have a prophetic calling, I was told to go get my ears checked out.

I was also told that you have to have money to be in ministry. While that is true to some degree, it is not absolute. God will make provision for the vision. This means if He called you to do it, the way has already been made for you to accomplish what He put in you to do. You just have to surrender and be willing to put in the work to obtain the promise or fulfill the vision. After all, faith without works is dead. We all have heard the phrase "Your labor is not in vain." Well, the term *labor* means "to put forth effort, to work hard, to work up a sweat, to push." If you think about a woman who is in labor and getting ready to deliver a baby, that woman's body is working, contracting, pushing the baby down, and preparing to deliver the baby. However, before that baby enters the world, that woman also has to push on her own and then eventually give one big final push before the baby leaves her body and is birthed into the world. That vision, assignment, or call that God has given you is like birthing a baby. It will require you to labor, to prepare, to work hard, push, and push some more until it is delivered. Once it is delivered, you then will have to nurture it, develop it, and grow it. Eventually you will be able to look at your baby, the fruit of your labor, and declare that your labor was not in vain. God can use you right where you are. I just want to encourage some-one. Sometimes people in high places can speak things into your life that can cost you your life. The person who spoke those things into my life has no idea it almost cost me my life. Be mindful of how you handle people in their valley/low season. You never know where they truly are in their mindset or mentality. A person can be near death or close to giving up. And how you handle them can be the difference between life or death for that person, his/her sanity or insanity, healing and deliverance, or setback. What is nothing to one person can mean everything to the next person.

I valued the church. I valued the opinions of leaders in the church. And the church broke me. The church sent me into a pit and into depression. To the point that I didn't want to get out of the bed. Honestly, I didn't want to live. I knew God had a mandate on my life, and I couldn't fulfill it. I didn't want to live. I would tell God, "I can't do what they won't allow me to do."

I gave my life to the church. And the church hurt me. When I say church, I am not making reference to everyone in the church. I am referring more specifically to the leaders. However, this does apply to anyone in the body of Christ. I was told that I was trying to emulate my leader when, in fact, all I wanted to do was serve God. I had to pray on this. Because I know that I am fearfully and wonderfully made. I know that I am unique and one of a kind. We may have some similarities, but there is no one just like you or me. We all are fearfully and wonderfully made. However, I do believe that after sitting under your leader for so long, eventually the oil that is on him or her should rub off on you. If it does not, then something is not right. Could it be you are not being poured into or spiritually fed? I do not share this story to bring shame to my pastor nor my church. I share my story because many people deal with church hurt and they turn their backs on the church. At some point, you have to grow beyond the viewpoint of people in your Christian walk. Why are you truly in church? Is it to serve God or people?

The Bible tells us that "God is a spirit: and they that worship Him must worship Him in spirit and in truth" (John 4:24). God had to deal with me concerning people. Despite how I felt about myself and what others may have thought, God called me. And I had to get up. When I first knew that God had called me to ministry, I shared the good news with a minister, and she was so happy. She gave me some words of wisdom and repeated them to me. She told me to make sure I do not drop the people. Ten years later, I have not forgotten those words. Those words were life to me in this walk and encouraged me to keep going. And when I felt like giving up, I would remember those words. We have the ability to encourage someone and build someone up with our words. Our words have power. We also have the ability to tear people down with our words, and though I have experienced both, I thank God for the woman of God who sowed that positive word into my life. Know that when you profess to be a Christian, and not only a Christian but to have any type of calling or assignment from God, it attracts the attention of the people. People will be watching you up close and from afar. Some to see you fail. Some to see if you will succeed. This is why it is so important to worship God in spirit and in truth and with a pure heart. What comes from the heart reaches the heart. It is also important that we as Christians live a life that lines up with our profession. The world is watching our lives. Everyone is not coming to the church. This is why we must let our light shine so that others may see our good works and glorify the Father who is in heaven. People already know their sins and shortcomings. But it is the love of Jesus that will draw men. Jesus said, "And I, if I be lifted up from the earth, will draw all men unto me. John 12:32" Jesus is love.

I began to pull away from our home church. My life was very busy outside of the church. I worked full-time, I was in and out of court battling for my children, and I could no longer afford the place I was living in nor my new vehicle. It was a huge sacrifice to travel back and forth to and from the church time-wise and financially. At the time, I lived forty-five minutes away from the church. And I was still grieving the loss of my father. Serving was truly a sacrifice for me. Not that I minded the sacrifice. I loved God, and I love to serve God's people. I also know that God honors your sacrifice. Though I began to pull away from my home church, I did not pull away from God. I had a discussion with my children, and we decided to start visiting other churches. While I was visiting different churches, I learned a few things. I learned that there were different doctrines out here. When I ran into certain things that just didn't sit right with me, God would remind me through scripture to "neglect not the gift that is in thee, which was given thee by prophecy, with the laying on of the hands of the presbytery" (1 Timothy 4:14).

I will never forget when my pastor laid hands on me at Bible study in February 2011 and I received the gift of the Holy Ghost. The Holy Ghost will lead and guide you into all truth. The Holy Spirit will cover and protect you if you listen to it. The Holy Spirit will keep you. Each time the Lord showed me this scripture, I took heed and remembered the teachings of my pastor. Also, as my family and I were visiting churches, we learned that the Lord can bless us no matter where we went. The Lord began to send people to bless my family. Not that we were looking for anything from anyone. I just believe God was reassuring me and my family that He was with us. This is why a true relationship with the Father (God) is so important. That relationship is obtained through prayer. No longer does a high priest have to enter into the holy of holies on behalf of the sins of the congregation. Because God sent his son Jesus Christ to die on the cross to bear the sins of the world, we all can now enter into the holies of holies for ourselves and ask for forgiveness of our sins. This is why we seal our prayers in the name of Jesus. No man can come to the Father except that he comes through Jesus Christ. Who are you going to serve? Are you going to serve God or man? Please know that no church is perfect and that leaders do make mistakes because they are also human. However, it is our job to pray for our leaders. You may not agree with everything that goes on in the church, how a church is ran, or the way you were treated by leadership. However, that doesn't necessarily mean that the leader or pastor doesn't have anything to say that can help you in this walk.

God may not be telling you to leave your church. Truthfully, you are going to find fault in every church you attend. God is telling us to be the church. Someone may be encouraged by your presence in the church. Your very presence may give someone the strength to keep going. This is why we go into the building: to testify, gain strength from one another, and then go out into the world and draw someone else. The Bible tells us in Hebrews 10:25 not to forsake the assembling of ourselves together. Maybe God is calling you to be a light even in the church. One thing I learned about God is that when you are faithful to Him, He will cause your name to be mentioned in rooms that you are not even in. God knows how to put you in the hearts of men and in the heart of your leader. I've seen Him do it. The Lord did it for me. He will reward you for your faithfulness and make His face shine upon you. Just pray about it. Prayer changes things. Sometimes all God wants you to do is to stand still and see the salvation of the Lord.

This may be the case for some of you. Know that as long as your heart is pure, God can bless you no matter where you are. And sometimes it may be okay to leave. Most of all, you want to be in the will of God whether you leave or stay. I chose to be transparent in this writing because I believe the only way we can really win souls for Jesus or reach the people is to be honest about struggle, our process, and our deliverance. People need to be able to see themselves in you and through my/your testimony and know that they can overcome. Scripture tells us that we overcome by the blood of the Lamb and by the word of our testimony (Revelation 12:11). Often we as Christians tend to hide our struggles and put on a face as if our life is perfect. I believe in this time when we are all wearing masks, God is unveiling the church. We all need Jesus. We all have areas in our lives in which we need to change or improve. We are not saved by our good works. We are saved because God loved us enough to send His only begotten son, Jesus, to die on the cross and bear the sins of the world. John 3:16 quotes, "For God so loved the world that he gave his only begotten son, that whosoever believed on Him, shall not perish but have everlasting life." No one was born saved. The Bible tells us "all have sinned and come short of the glory of God" (Romans 3:23).

I believe that God can use anyone. He has no respect of a person. This means that salvation is available to everyone. God does not choose you based on your past, present, social status, popularity, finances (or lack thereof), or mistakes. God will use whom He pleases to get the glory out of their lives. God can use the homeless. God can deliver the drug addict or drug dealer and put him in the pulpit. God can use a prostitute. God can use those whom man deemed unworthy. What an awesome God we serve.

When God shows you who you are in Him, believe Him. I believe God. So far, almost everything the Lord has shown me concerning me has come to pass. I believe God for the rest. Though He did not show me the process, He has kept His promise. Every promise that He made, it will come to pass. God will not go back on His word. He will never leave you. He will never forsake you. He will never turn his back on you.

God didn't let me give up. He sent people from the outside of my church, people from other churches, to encourage me. He sent strangers to encourage me. A prime example of how God can use anyone is the homeless.

Consider the homeless; they have nowhere to lay their head but somehow find a way to encourage others and thank God for what they do have, life. I have received encouragement from the homeless and strangers. That word was sometimes as simple as "Jesus loves you." I knew Jesus loved me. But it didn't always feel like it. Sometimes I wondered, "Where are you, God?" Sometimes I wanted to throw in the towel. But then the Lord would send someone, a stranger or even an angel, to encourage me. Yes, I believe in angels. That's why we have to be careful of how we treat people, who we look down upon, and who we are rejecting. You could be entertaining an angel. Not only that He would send someone along for me to help. Even in my low place, I had to help someone else. I would often go back to God and ask, "How can I encourage someone else when I'm going through something myself?" But that was the call that God had for my life. I couldn't give up.

I heard a profound minister of the gospel say that you cannot minister to her if you are on Section 8. I just want to encourage somebody. God can use you right where you are. I am a single mother who grew up in the projects and was on Section 8. And it did not stop God from calling me. We have to be very careful of how we judge people because the very person you are looking down on can be the person God uses to draw or save your loved ones, to lay hands on you or a family member so they become healed. Sometimes God will allow you to experience a low place so that when you receive greater, you can appreciate it. I am sharing this because there is a misconception within the body of Christ that you have be of a particular status to be used by God. Jesus did not come to save the rich. He came for the lost. On my worst day, if I can help somebody, then my living is not in vain. I have sat in the workplace and among church members and listened to them talk about people who came from the projects and who were on Section 8, not knowing they were sitting with one, me. You cannot always look at a person and tell what they have been through. While I was thankful for the assistance, God knows it was not my desire to stay there or depend on it. I've worked all my life. But through prayer, faith, and obedience to the will of God, God has moved me from faith to faith and from glory to glory. I am forever grateful for that. God has kept His promise to me. He said in His Word, "I have never seen the righteous forsaken nor his seed begging for bread." God will supply your every need. God has made so many ways for me and opened so many doors for me. They definitely are not all listed in this book. But know that prayer is the key to the kingdom and faith unlocks the door. When you step out on faith and begin to move in the things that God has shown you and promised you, your faith will move mountains. Your faith unlocks the blessings and favor of God.

I want to encourage any young mother, single mother, father, and anyone who is struggling with life issues, poverty, bad relationships, being mishandled, being misunderstood, feeling depressed, and being alone. You can make it. With Jesus on your side, you can make it. Your struggles are real. But God is bigger than your struggle. Where you are is not your final destination. You are in your process. Poverty will not have the final say in your life. Disappointment will not have the final say in your life. People will not have the final say in your life. Stand on the promises of God. Your gift will make room for you. If God said it, believe it and be willing to go through the process. Your anointing is in the process. Your growth is in the process. Your perseverance is in the process. The oil comes from the process. I choose to stand on the promises of God. When man says no, God at any time can say yes. What God has for you, it is for you.

Every closed door has brought me closer to the place where God wants me to be. When one season of ministry ended, another began. When I stopped fighting the process, the doors began to swing open. It is my prayer that through this writing, someone is being restored. Don't give up on God.

CHAPTER 11

The Promise

By now you may be wondering, why I titled this book *Standing on the Promises of God*. The answer is because God gave me a vision. God made me a promise. Just as He has given many of you. However, God did not show me how I would get there. I had to go through a process. Through the process, I learned to trust God more and more. I learned to move at the command of God. I learned to obey the voice of God.

Romans 8:28 states, "And we know that all things work together for good to them that love God, to them who are the called according to his purpose." I love this scripture because it reminds me that no matter what I go through (the good, the bad, and the ugly), it's all working together to bring me into the promise God has for me. I know that it's all working for my good. The lies, the hurt, the disappointment, the rejection, the isolation, the wait, the closed doors, it's all working for my good. I've had to minister while broken, battered, scarred, hurting, battling. I've ministered while fighting for my children. I've ministered knowing that I wasn't liked or favored and looked down upon. I've ministered while going through bad relationships, including family. "Why?" you ask? Because God made me a promise. If I just hold out and keep the faith, He would take care of my children and me. He would bless me with houses I did not build. So no matter what I'm going through, I hold on to the promise. God promised that He will bless my children and my children's children if they would keep the covenant, obey God, and keep Him first: Deuteronomy 11:13–21 quotes:

And it shall come to pass, if ye shall hearken diligently unto my commandments which I command you this day, to love the Lord your God, and to serve him with all your heart and with all your soul,

That I will give you the rain of your land in his due season, the first rain and the latter rain, that thou mayest gather in thy corn, and thy wine, and thine oil.

And I will send grass in thy fields for thy cattle, that thou mayest eat and be full.

Take heed to yourselves, that your heart be not deceived, and ye turn aside, and serve other gods, and worship them;

Therefore, shall ye lay up these my words in your heart and in your soul, and bind them for a sign upon your hand, that they may be as frontlets between your eyes.

And ye shall teach them your children, speaking of them when thou sittest in thine house, and when thou walkest by the way, when thou liest down, and when thou risest up.

And thou shalt write them upon the door posts of thine house, and upon thy gates:

That your days may be multiplied, and the days of your children, in the land which the Lord sware unto your fathers to give them, as the days of heaven upon the earth.

I know that God is going to bring me to it. I expect God to do it. Stand on the word of God. Stand on the promises of God, for the promises of God are "Yea" and "Amen."

As you can see, I quoted quite a few scriptures throughout the book. This is because the promises of God are the Word of God. The word of God changes not. "Thy word is a lamp unto my feet and a light unto my path" (Psalm:119:105). "Thy word have I hid in my heart that I might not sin against thee" (Psalm 119:11). The Word of God will lead you into all truth. The Word of God will lead you into the promise of God. I am standing on the Word of God. I am standing on the promises of God.

ABOUT THE AUTHOR

LaTonya is a single mother of four children. She finds joy in raising her children in the fear of the Lord while raising them to be productive citizens.

LaTonya is a faithful member of an amazing church in Chicago where she serves on various ministries including the choir, praise team, pastoral care, and outreach ministry.

She holds an associate's degree in general business from Malcolm X College and a bachelor of science degree in technical management with an emphasis in small business management and entrepreneurship from DeVry University. She is also a member Sigma Beta Delta, an international honor society for business management and administration.

LaTonya has a career in public service as a human services caseworker.

She has a passion for serving others and encouraging others to walk in their God-given purpose and ultimately reach their destiny.

You may contact her through the following:

- Facebook: Author LaTonya R Forrest

- Instagram: latonyarforrest

- Email: LForrest24@yahoo.com

Other writings include the bestseller *A Purpose Driven Woman: 14 Memoirs on Becoming Fearless and Intentional* (coauthored by LaTonya R. Forrest) available at http://bit.ly/LaTonyaForrest.

www.ingramcontent.com/pod-product-compliance
Lightning Source LLC
Chambersburg PA
CBHW030922040326
40505CB00044B/830